THE AMERICAN POETRY REVIEW/HONICKMAN FIRST BOOK PRIZE

The Honickman Foundation is dedicated to the support of projects that promote spiritual growth and creativity, education and social change. At the heart of the mission of the Honickman Foundation is the belief that creativity enriches contemporary society because the arts are powerful tools for enlightenment, equity and empowerment, and must be encouraged to effect social change as well as personal growth. A current focus is on the particular power of photography and poetry to reflect and interpret reality, and, hence, to illuminate all that is true.

The annual American Poetry Review/Honickman First Book Prize offers publication of a book of poems, a $3,000 award, and distribution by Copper Canyon Press through Consortium. Each year a distinguished poet is chosen to judge the prize and write an introduction to the winning book. The purpose of the prize is to encourage excellence in poetry, and to provide a wide readership for a deserving first book of poems. *Throwing the Crown* is the twenty-first book in the series.

WINNERS OF THE AMERICAN POETRY REVIEW/
HONICKMAN FIRST BOOK PRIZE

THROWING THE CROWN

JACOB SAENZ

Throwing the Crown

The American Poetry Review
Philadelphia

Cover art: Krista Franklin
Book design and composition: VJB/Scribe
Distribution by Copper Canyon Press/Consortium

Library of Congress Control Number: 2018943185

ISBN 978-0-9833008-6-1 cloth
ISBN 978-0-9833008-7-8 paper

9 8 7 6 5 4 3 2 FIRST EDITION

for my mother Juana and my brothers Marc,
Dave and Manny

Contents

III

Introduction by Gregory Pardlo

What if one of Gwendolyn Brooks' seven young men at the Golden Shovel pool hall decided he wasn't particularly interested in "lurking late" or "jazzing June"? Let's imagine his leaving school one day was, at least for him, a fleeting act of rebellion, and that otherwise he attended school regularly. What if, instead of succumbing to the collective fate foretold in the final couplet of that famous poem by Brooks, "We Real Cool," this young man—let's call him "Jacob"—applied himself in school and became a poet? How might Jacob rewrite Brooks' poem? How might he expand on Brooks' literary estate? Brooks' poem elegantly renders a narrative of futility and seeming hopelessness. We still often use that narrative to explain generational cycles of poverty and violence. How would Jacob address that narrative today?

More than a thought experiment, Jacob Saenz's debut collection *Throwing the Crown* quietly defies the old narratives that portray young men in cities like Chicago as anonymous statistics and cautionary tales. At a time when our politicians actively vilify and scapegoat immigrant communities in general, but none more so than Mexican Americans, Saenz leads us away from fearmongering politicians.

It's true for everyone: the conditions that surround us can no more define us than a packet of seasoning for sale in the "Ethnic Foods aisle" that "create[s] a taste muy authentico." Still, even the well-meaning among us slip into the language of essentialism that separates "those people" into a distinctly different category of human being no matter who "those people" may be. We are conditioned to distance ourselves through such unexamined language, and to overlook the individual experiences of people for whom, as in this case, street violence is as ever-present as delays in public transportation. With slogans and institutional jargon, we play a kind of rhetorical shell game equivalent to offering (at best!) empty "thoughts and prayers" for the latest otherwise remediable source of outrage.

Because Saenz refuses to do so, his poems won't allow us to sentimentalize the structural violence and poverty many of them depict. His poems demand to be read in the full context of the American experience, and thus the American literary tradition, and not as sociological records of a benighted population.

Like Brooks, Saenz is both woke and deeply committed to craft, which is to say his poems call our attention equally to the beauty of their form. Saenz's skillful and rich lyricism is abundant with internal rhyme, staccato anapests and dactyls, and athletic extended metaphors. The poem "Shootaround," for example, seems to signpost a number of social ills at once until we realize this is kind of the point. The entire poem is an extended metaphor (and not merely in the sense that all poems are extended metaphors). The story is simple: a boy shoots hoops on a school blacktop. Saenz adorns this humble narrative in such a way that demonstrates how much our experience is shaped and filtered through political discourse. Saenz's first-person speaker "runs onto the lot" of a school in a town where a neighboring school celebrates "Wigger Day," and the speaker "start[s] shooting/ around shirtless." That line break invokes both basketball and school tragedies, and it shows us how easily we can hold those two ideas in mind at once. One of the arguments the poem goes on to make is that all of the conversations we hold separately, conversations about mass shootings, police violence, racism, mass incarceration among other concerns—these are not separate conversations at all.

What child isn't "at risk," the poems seem to ask, which makes the coming-of-age story that emerges over the course of *Throwing the Crown* unsettlingly familiar. Childhood games reproduce the indifferent logic of institutions designed to sequester people within real and imaginary limits. Guns and gunplay (what a word!) turn up explicitly in poems like *"Traviesos"* as a couple of fifteen-year olds are threatened by "a whistle / of metal & flame." That danger is more subtly invoked elsewhere. Take away the guns, and you get an average working class American boyhood full of baseball and hoops. As if it could be that simple. What childhood these days is not menaced by the presence of guns in the community?

To "throw the crown" is to make the hand signal that represents the Latin Kings. It identifies the signaler as a member of that street gang. Throwing the crown is a semaphore of power expressed where power is most precariously defined, and yet the crown abounds in these poems. In this deeply patriarchal culture, the crown represents a force that has a long and destructive history. Agents of that crown, for Saenz, are gangbangers and cops alike. Its power is capricious, symbolized by the "pit bull bitch" described in the poem "Chula": "a butt-ugly mutt w/a mug bit-to-shit / from fighting in pits as a pup." The crown diverts its subjects with beer and Cheetos. The crown has the power to protect and to harm, and is always at a distance that is just shy of "safe." The crown exists in the midst of a threatened democracy. How would a hypothetical poet capture the complexities and the absurdities of this moment? Fortunately for us, there is no need to guess. In *Throwing the Crown*, Jacob Saenz has penned an American lyric, and has reinvigorated language for our time.

THROWING THE CROWN

I

Blue Line Incident

He was just some coked-out,
crazed King w/crooked teeth
& a tear drop forever falling,
fading from his left eye, peddling
crack to passengers or crackheads
passing as passengers on a train
chugging from Chicago to Cicero,
from the Loop through K-Town:
Kedzie, Kostner, Kildare.

I was just a brown boy in a brown shirt,
head shaven w/fuzz on my chin,
staring at treetops & rooftops
seated in a pair of beige shorts:
a badge of possibility—a Bunny
let loose from 26th street,
hopping my way home, hoping
not to get shot, stop after stop.

But a 'banger I wasn't & he wasn't
buying it, sat across the aisle from me:
Do you smoke crack?
Hey, who you ride wit'?
Are you a D'?
Let me see—throw it down then.

I hesitate then fork three fingers down
then boast about my block,
a recent branch in the Kings growing tree;
the boys of 15th and 51st, I say,
they're my boys, my friends.

I was fishing for a life-
saver & he took, hooked him in
& had him say goodbye like we was boys
& shit when really I should've
gutted that fuck w/the tip
of my blue ballpoint.

Evolution of My Skin

Born nine pounds brown
like grandpa's skin after a shift
of picking fruit off trees

in a field blazed by ultra-
violet rays. Then I fade
to a lighter shade, a color

closer to mother's minus
her freckles & the lone mole
kissed on her cheek.

My skin turns its tint again
my eyes read as brown but no,
olive according to agents

at a commercial audition
when I was nine years old,
black & white headshots

of black & white boys
dotting waiting room walls.
Little brother, born early

& light w/the dark features
of his father, calls me *Chocolate*
or *Hershey* growing up–

I thought *Caramel*
a tastier word. At fifteen,
I worked a summer shirtless

under the sun assembling
wooden fences & patios,
smearing dirt on my skin

—a blazing burnt brown
closer to my coworkers
born on the other side

of a defended fence.
Now I stay brownest
on my arms & neck

& face, leaving my legs
& torso sun-thirsting
& fading under faded jeans

& boxers, which cover
the darkest parts
that never see the sun.

Cops & Robbers

When nights & streets were free
of gangbangers posted on corners
like stop signs halting our play,
we kids from the block took on roles

of cops & robbers patrolling
the hood for a sense of order.
As the oldest kid, I picked out
boys lined up against the side

of my house—a row of potential
thieves & crooks shooting me
hopeful looks to choose them
for our local crime syndicate.

The cops counted to fifty
while we robbers ran through
the block, spreading out
like rats & roaches. Sometimes

I'd pair up w/the smallest kid
as we ran down dark alleys,
gangways & yards unguarded
by locks or dogs, looking

for hiding spots: behind
garbage cans, under porches
inside some stranger's hallway
where we stayed put in shadows.

We came out of cover in the name
of freedom, brushing against bushes
& buildings as we snuck to front
porch steps—the jail cell

w/faces of the captured
pressed between banister bars,
waiting for a breakout that came
w/a slap of our hands, a tag

of liberation that cost us captivity
by guards on duty who couldn't
catch us all, just the fresh meat.
Then we would sit anxiously,

crying out for help w/our arms
outstretched, hoping to be tagged,
wanting that freedom just so
the chase could begin again.

Chula

Chula the white pit bull bitch on the block
who barked at passersby from her backyard.

Chula a butt-ugly mutt w/a mug bit-to-shit
from fighting in pits as a pup, little pink pocks
dotting her face like gunshots.

Chula mother of a litter of full-breeds to be sold
only to have them stolen in the night
causing a fight between sets of brothers
on the block w/rocks & sewer tops chucked,
cop cars called in to quell the blood spill
when a blade was drawn & swung.

Chula one day snapped & lock-jawed on
her owner's arm & hung on when sprayed
w/a garden hose & hit w/a stick
like a piñata w/no candy to give.

Chula one night crushed a cat's legs in her mouth
& tossed it under a truck like a chew toy
where it played dead & stayed until morning
when it was rescued by Chula's owners.

Chula I was too scared to pet, too scarred
from an attack by a stray dog fucking
in the middle of the alley I walked down
to get home as a first grader.

Chula sniffed the air around me,
sweat pooling on my forehead
& growled whenever I neared.

Demon

Back when corner stores
on each end of the block
were owned by men named
Muhammed & Ahmed then
changed to Mike & Mark
in the name of capitalism,
a new brand of snacks
stacked the shelves of urban
minimarts, targeted for poor
hungry bodies—Flamin'
Hot Cheetos by Frito-Lay.
On the bag, a little devil stood
pitchforked & pointy-tailed
in our land of pitchforks & crowns.
We feasted on these salty & spicy
corn sticks like a pack of hyenas
cackling over a cracked open
carcass of antelope, our tongues
& fingers turning crimson
as we tagged each other red
on the playground. We finished
a bag & craved more of the fire
& crunch we munched on
for breakfast, lunch & dinner.
We ran back to the store to score
more of the product we craved
whether we paid for it w/coins
or snatched a bag off the shelf
stealth-like & walked into streets
where we opened up & unleashed
the fiend who licked & sucked
our blood-like fingers clean.

Mad About Cows

I've eaten part of a cow's heart
to become a part of the past,
of tío & his talk of grandpa's
love of tacos of the heart,
the eyes & brain, the parts
of a cow that make one mad.

I've held a heart hacked to chunks
& cooked on the grill in the backyard,
a warm corn tortilla cradling parts
of artery too hard to chew through
w/teeth not trained for the toughness
of the meat, the organ that once beat
in the body of a beast who feasted on grass.

I've tried to taste a piece of the past,
of abuelo's craving for tacos de corazon,
ojos y cerebro pero two bites was enough
to feel what I felt it must've been like for him,
the flavor & fullness, the forever chewing.

Sonnet of the Dead

When there's no more room in hell, the dead will
walk the earth.

DAWN OF THE DEAD

We don't know when the horde will come to feast,
when the dead will dig their way out the dirt
& lurch along in throngs reeking the streets
w/the smell of hell's expelled come to earth.

We can't prepare for their hunger of flesh,
the terror of teeth tearing meat off bone.
Better to die than be bit but it's best
to live, to blast a hole right in their dome.

Best to load up on canned goods & big guns,
board up windows, sharpen the machete
& stay fit for when we must split & run
toward our rescue by air or by sea.

We're built to survive, outlast the dead's
desire for what's buried deep in our heads.

The Lot as Baseball Field

The diamond is a rectangle
of mangled weeds & weak grass
growing in patches w/a strip
of concrete down the middle
of the lot, the stone remnant
that once divided two houses
now housing ghosts & children.
I stand on the mound, a line
somewhere along the gangway
we deem an eight year old's equivalent
of ninety feet. I clutch the baseball,
fingering the seams & threading
as Miguel stands ready at home plate
—a slab of grey stone set down
at the base of his feet. He swings
& slices the air w/Peace-
maker, my older brother's bat,
the name carved into it like lovers'
initials. (The same tool I once used
to make peace w/César
when he slapped my head
& giggle-pedaled away on his bike.
I chased him like Captain Caveman
& brought the piece of wood down
on his back & ran for home
where mom tagged me out w/the heel
of her chancla, putting me on the DL.)
I wind-up & release my best Nolan Ryan
throw, mimicking the captured movements
on his baseball cards, my lips
smacked together w/force & intent.

Miguel swings & smashes the ball right
back to my chest, a mini cannon straight
to the hull of a ship & I sink down,
losing air as water bursts from my eyes.
Miguel rushes over & rubs my back
as I cry-heave & he's sorry as he places
Peacemaker at my feet, which rolls
towards the ball like a stick of dynamite.

Bait

The mother sends her ten-year old
        boy into the bar to fish out
                his father—a pool shark chalking
        up his cue stick, wetting his lips
on dark bottles of beer, burning
        the tips of his fingers from a dying
                scroll of brown & crimson leaves.

She waits while her boy swims
        past stools of pants & skirts, the blaring
                of trumpets & tubas from a jukebox
        glowing under a cursive neon sign
towards the open collar in the back,
        the mustached man laying dollars down
                for the next game, the next beer for
        the brunette sharing his cigarette.

The boy enters the smoke
        & closes in on the pool table,
                remembering his lines about rent
        & food, the clothes he & his little
brother need. The same words
        he used weeks ago in the same
                bar, a routine rehearsed & refined.
        An act the boy is sick of & coughs
loudly enough to draw attention
        away from the game & women,
                the hook & line stuck firmly
        in his boy mouth no matter
the struggle to spit it loose & free.

The father sees the boy & exhales
        a drag of smoke into the ceiling
                fan, slams down the bitterness
        of beer. He follows the boy
like a fish he wishes to swallow,
        to wipe his name off the food
                chain—another mouth to throw
        chum bits of a paycheck to.

Outside the bar the boy dangles
        from his mother's hand & listens
                to the slurring & blurring of Spanish
        & English—*Y cuando vienes a casa?*
Ya estas drunk *y el* rent *es debido.*
        Señora, señora, señora, listen...—
        But the boy already knows
        what comes next—the splitting
open of a wallet, a glut of dollar bills
        spilling out for the bills at home.
                The father dives back into the bar,
        his cue stick needing more chalk,
his tongue thirsting for more
        bitter hops. The mother reels
                her boy to her hand & places
        him back in the tackle box
of home.

Shootaround

I run onto the lot
of the local school's
outdoor basketball
court & start shooting
around shirtless,
burning my shoulders
under a sizzling
July sunset. Alone,
I focus on form
& follow-through, bending
knees, pointing my right
elbow toward the basket,
my arm a goose's
neck upon release.
The ball echoes
off walls w/each
bounce, the chain
net rattles crisply
w/each swish.
Above, I see birds circle
over trees on a cliff
overlooking the court
like skybox seating.
Midway through shooting
a white cop rushes
onto school grounds.
I think *Game Over*
because I'm a brown body
on a blacktop in a town
where a school celebrates
"Wigger Day" w/white kids

donning doo rags & baggy
pants, their heads drenched
in fake dreads & cultural
appropriation. Instead the cop
turns a corner & walks down
an aisle surrounding
the school. I fling
a few more shots
which clank off
the rim as sweat
slides down my face
& chest as he heads toward
trees & bushes to conceal
his movements. I glance up
& witness a hawk
swooping deep
into green leaves
for a prey I cannot see.

Showering

Towels wrapped tight around
our waists, we walked slowly
across the locker room's wet

tiled floor where we unwound
the cloth cover & concealed
what we didn't want to reveal

w/sixth-grade hands cupping
& cradling our cocks & balls:
a walling off of our privates

for lack of privacy walls.
We looked towards the floor
& rarely at each other, full

of soap foam & shame.
In between lather & rinse,
I glimpsed Adrian's lush

pubes, a hairy crown above
his penis while I bared
mostly skin. Michael

walked around freely,
openly showing his cut
member while mine hung

cloaked. Drying off, Charles
talked of his dick buried
beneath his belly fat

which he lifted to show me
his shaft small & pink
unlike my brown shrinkage

after a shower—a balled up
boy afraid of growing
& showing his hooded man-

-hood in locker rooms
where I toweled off sweat
even after a showering.

The Macho

How old was I—10? 12?—when I saw
them in the kitchen hallway,
her body pressed against the wall
by the fading blue *L-O-V-E*

inked on knuckles clutching
mother's throat? I emerged from
my room where GI Joes fought
each other w/unclenched hands,

my fists balled up, fear
shaking my body into an idea
of masculinity. I would fight
my stepfather, drunk blood

of my little brother who stood
in the doorway crying
Papi, please let her go!
My blood blitzed like The Hulk

& I wished for gamma strength
in order to smash my stepfather's
skull & brain until what remained
was too explicit for the paneled

pages of comics where violence
was all bright colors & bold letters.
I wanted to be the Macho
Man she would call me when I walked

around shirtless, flexing non-existent
muscles. I imagined myself flying
high off a turnbuckle w/an elbow
crashing on the crown

of his head, knocking him
down for the count: 1-2-3!
But she ordered us back to bed
as he looked past us & unfastened

herself from his grip, our lips
still quivering, my body shivering.
I morphed back to the boy
I was, powerless & pec-less.

Silence swallowed the night.
I woke to see my stepfather snoring
on the couch, mother in the kitchen,
chorizo & eggs sizzling in the pan.

This Never Happened

You & your boys walk home
from school & cut down the alley
behind the varnish factory
at the end of your block —
four sophomores who ain't soft,
looking hard in hairnets & Starter jackets,
the cool you exude so heavy it drags
your extra-baggy black Dickies
halfway off your ass even w/a belt on.

A banger in a blue Buick drives by
& flashes the crown w/his left hand.
You throw it up right
back at him cuz you're a wannabe,
a gonnabe, got brothers & cousins
who were born to be Kings.
When he stops the car & calls you
over to the driver side door,
you move like you're kin
long lost & now found again.

But the reunion ends when he pulls
the gun out & presses it to your neck,
the .22's cold steel kills the feeling
of family & your boys look on
spooked, one ready to run, the others
searching for a rock or bottle to throw.

He asks who you ride w/,
what gang you & your boys ran
& when you tell him none, *I ain't*

shit, we ain't shit & are 'bout to shit
your pants cuz of the pistol & his black
leather sleeve still gripping your neck,
you remember the leather coat
you asked your mom to get you
for Christmas like the boys at school.

Now you feel the fool, tricked
by a Two-Six throwing up
the crown w/the wrong hand
to check what set you claim
& cuz he's an O.G. & sees
you're nothing but a shorty
scared & shivering in his arms,
he warns you & your boys not to bang,
not to hang on the corner
cuz if he ever saw you he'd shoot you.
Then he lets you loose & drives off
slow like a cop who busts you
for driving over the speed limit.

Your boys crowd you like you've fallen
from the sky & you tell 'em you alright,
frightened but forget him, fuck him
but don't tell your brothers,
pretend like this never happened.

The Lot as Boxing Ring

Quique & I were given gloves
inside the ring of gravel & weeds:
one pair a classic boxer's red,
one green, white & red w/a brown
eagle eating a snake on the pricks
of a cactus plant, making a punch
sting like a strike of wing & talon.

Our boys laced us up w/Quique taking
the Mexican pair due to his fluency
in a tongue I struggled w/, the cost
of second-generation assimilation.

We thought we were the second coming
of Julio César Chavez, the boxer
my Mexican stepfather hotboxed pay-per-view
fights for, getting upgrade packages
from cable guys seduced by Spanish
& offers of beer during installation.
We felt we had chins built to withstand
hits of stone fists, to stick & move across
the ring using ropes as leverage—the chain
link fence around Armando's blue home,
the fading yellow siding of our building.

When the bell rung from the tongue
of someone's mouth, we swung
our arms like drowners in a deep
sea, neither of us knowing how
to throw a proper punch, to knock
a kid's head back & make them

bleed or black-eyed & bruised.
In our flailing of failed hits,
I landed a jab smack on his face,
his nose spilling twin rivers of red
he wiped clean w/the white part
of his glove while his blood
blended into the color of my own.

GTA: San Andreas/Berwyn (or, "Grove Street, bitch!")

after Mary Jo Bang

I play on Grove Street,
live on Grove Avenue.

Find me in the streets dressed
in greens like groves.

On the avenue, I'm a blue
jeans type of guy.

In the streets, never leave
home w/out my 9mm.

On the avenue, always carry
my pen & wine key, in case

some fool blows his cork.
My uzi sings songs in

the streets—*ratta-tat-tat*.
Birds chirp-chirp-chirp

in trees on the avenue.
Rolling down the street

w/my lady—what she wanna do?
"Let's do a drive by."

Rushing down the avenue
w/my baby: "I'm hungry.

Let's do drive-thru."
I'll punch punks purple & blue

in the streets, bleed 'em w/bullets.
On the avenue, I'll leave punching

to punks dressed in blues, reds,
etcetera & accelerate home.

Latin Immortal Gangstas

Before Kings came in on lowrider chariots
w/banners of black & gold draped
over their bodies & laid claim to corners
by posting pawns, we believed the block
belonged to us, a crew of boys who outgrew
games of ding-dong ditch & ditched high school
classes to smoke weed & play Playstation
at Paul's place while Westside Connection's
"Bow Down" boomed from radio. & we bowed down
in front of the TV controlling our desires
w/joysticks to adjust the camera's angle
until a close-up of Lara Croft's
polygonal breast appeared like an arrow
aimed at freshman hearts. In another room,
some watched scrambled porn lying belly down
on beds to hide hard-ons whenever
a distorted nipple or penis flashed
on the screen like lightening. The day
a mouse scurried across the living room
Carlos' Converse sneaker became hammer,
smashing it dead on the rug but not dead
enough for us who took the body in-
to the alley w/a can of Aqua
Net hairspray & a lighter to ignite
laughter as we watched the body burn
until glee turned to shame.
                              After a game
of basketball on Juan's concrete court
where Victor yelled *Kobe!* after every shot,
we decided to let fists fly & flail
on our backs & arms w/a sprinkling

of shin kicks until we reached
the three-minute mark & marked ourselves
Latin Immortal Gangstas 4 Life.
We posted up on corners like cardboard
cutouts of gang life: hairnets hitched
to our skulls, black & brown clothes
sagging off our asses, our fingers coiling
to passing cars leaking oil & banda music.
The day Hugo bicycled to the bank
& returned w/an ear blooming a withered
red rose from a broken bottle, we vowed
revenge against La Raza, those cloaked
in red, white & green like the flag
of our mothers' & fathers' heartland.
We gathered up bricks & bats to strike back
& risked war w/no army behind us,
a squad of eight deep w/knees shaking
as we marched to the corner of Central
Federal Banking & found the spot
abandoned, ghosts in their place, a mother
wheeling a cart of groceries back
from Supermercado Garza. We tagged
LRK & LIGN on a garage, the letters
crooked & dripping paint, waiting
to be coated over w/another layer
of letters by wayward boys believing
their block & mark never fading.

II

The Bachelor Attends a Wedding

This is what the living do, those who believe
in public displays of affection. They wear matching
suits & dresses of purple & gray & white. They stand
at altars, read from a big book under a holy roof
& birdshit-stained glass windows. They exchange
vows while I check my phone for Facebook updates,
hoping someone likes my cat photo. They hire
a DJ, a photographer, caterers to cart around
plates of chicken & pasta, mashed potatoes
& scoops of vanilla ice cream, my favorite.
I sit at a table on the bride's side w/her brother
dressed in a soldier's uniform. He's my brother
from another mother, my best man
if I were to ever marry, to get over the wariness
I feel about white dresses & long aisles.
During the bouquet toss, all singles ladies
form a crowd & wait for flowers to fall
from the sky. The garter fling forces me
to bring my nephew amongst the bachelors
& use his body to deflect the lace projectile.
A groomsman catches it & stuffs it
into his mouth like a bone. I tell my nephew
we're all animals & he wants more ice cream.
I talk to my brother about wrestling, the new
champion & we can't wait for the next main
event, even though the outcome is fixed.
I walk over to a photo-booth & take a picture
of myself wearing an eye-patch & gangster hat.
I give it to the bride before I leave. I hug her
goodbye & I feel her body like a tree,
her roots reaching deeper into the earth.

The Bachelor Makes Dinner

I preheat the oven & tear open
a box of frozen pizza, tossing aside
the brand name & shrink wrap
like a gift on Xmas morning.
I stick my hand into the heat, singe
my skin on hot metal & know
dinner is ready to cook. I place
the pizza on the middle rack, set
the timer & wait for the buzz to get me
up off the couch where I watch
old episodes of a comedy show
& chuckle along w/the laugh track.
I pull the pizza out the oven. The cheese
bubbles, the sausage sizzles. I drizzle
Louisiana hot sauce on a slice
of butter-crusted grease & greatness.
I take a bite & my heart dies a little.

The Bachelor Takes Out the Trash

I toss the ravaged remains of my savage
single life into a plastic drawstring bag:
banana peels & pistachio shells, nail clippings,
pubic hair trimmings, chewed chicken bones,
the shards of a *Wake the Fuck Up!* coffee mug
& empty bottle upon empty bottle of bitter
dark elixirs piled together like the discards
of a failed alchemist. Potion of Revelry.
Potion of Longing. Potion of Flatulence.
Potion of Impotence. Potion of Forgetting.
I only have so much space for all this waste.
The bag begins to tear at the edges & leaks a dark
fluid like a busted condom, which is also inside
the sack leaking life. I hurry the down the stairs
into the backyard where a garden grows vegetables
for the upstairs neighbor's mouth. Meanwhile,
I eat my genetically-engineered veggies straight
from the can, thanks given to ConAgra Foods
& their investors! At the dumpster, I open the lid
& throw in the bag like a body, the corpse of
the person I was. I look towards the garbage bin
next door, the one belonging to a young married couple
& I see the rump of a fat raccoon climbing in.
It'll find the diapers of their bratty kids, the small
bags of shit from their dog who never shuts up
but also the tossed out leftovers of a home-
cooked meal—roasted lemongrass free-range
chicken & organic asparagus served over brown
rice w/a side of sea-salted kale chips baked
in olive oil. I think on my dinner of peanut butter
& Funyuns & am glad it's gluten-free.

The raccoon emerges w/a half-eaten apple
in its thieving little hands & looks my way.
I return its gaze & say, *You'll find nothing worth
scavenging here. Better stick to the garbage of marriage.*

The Bachelor Attends Another Wedding

When I reach for the suit I've already worn
to two previous weddings, I feel like a janitor
about to don his uniform to clock in & scrub
the walls & toilet, to mop the floor
w/a bucket of tears & Pine-sol.
The tie's knot is still intact, loose
at the neck & ready to slip on
& tighten like (what else?) a noose.
When I look in the mirror, I see a body fit
for a coffin, the lid open to welcome
bereaved hands to touch one last time.
After the ceremony, I make my way
to the bar & order two gin & tonics,
one for me, the other for my lover
who exists only in the ether. I snack
on many mini crab cakes & bruschetta
spread on bread like bits of placenta.
During the dance, I find myself swaying
w/the maid of honor garbed in green,
the hemline of dress swallowing her feet,
giving the illusion of floatation, my hands
anchors at her waist. She tells me
of the horse she owns, the ranch
she works at up in the mountains.
I imagine us riding bareback together
over a field of cosmos & bachelor buttons,
my arms hitched across her stomach.
I'm afraid to fall & face-
plant, afraid to land hard on
my ass & stain my suit w/purple
pollen & fresh fertilizer. At the end

of the night, I ask for her number
& she hands me a souvenir vase
w/a single flower in it, the water
already tossed down a drain.

The Bachelor Screws in a Light Bulb

I flick the switch & remain in the dark.
It's time to replace the old way of seeing
w/a new light. I climb the ladder w/a box
of fluorescents, the essence of which uses
less energy & lasts longer but when I twist
the compact lamp into its socket, its helical
design is a pig's tail hanging from the ceiling,
a filthy end to such cost saving efficiency.
It's eco-friendly glow casts about the room
& bounces off the couch & coffee table,
the ottoman I rest my feet on like an Ottoman
stretching his legs on the back of a slave.
Oh, how I'll miss the feel of the old
bulb in my palm, the curved container
of so much heat & so little radiance.
What am I to do w/this used shell
of light? The right thing is recycle,
pass the glass onto a new shape, a lens
to let more light through. Instead I let
it fall to the floor & crash into shards
I sweep up w/the dust, the collected dead
flesh from days past—trash to be burned
by a fire bright enough to read by.

The Bachelor Watches *The Bachelor*

I sit on the couch & witness my life
projected on a screen—I am white
w/a chiseled, dimpled chin & no lips.
I'm a farmer who lives alone in a loft
& not a lowly office worker who lives
w/a roommate in an apartment where
dust balls decorate the floors & walls
& the ceiling rings w/children's feet
running back & forth like baby bulls.
I am crazy enough to be a contestant
on a show where I'm contractually obligated
to propose to a woman who believes
in a heteronormative, patriarchal
idea of what a family should be.
At the end of every episode, I offer
roses to those I wish to make out w/more
& take out on pre-packaged romantic dates
I could never afford on my bachelor budget.
For example: a date in a castle, a glass
slipper prop, a clock winding its way
down to midnight. My date & I sip
champagne, chat & eat then we dance
to a live orchestra led by a maestro
who wishes he were dead. A giant screen appears
& plays a clip of a live-action Cinderella movie
w/Prince Charming played by an actor
I've seen slaughter & behead a soldier
like clipping the head off a rose.
In real life, my dates consist of dinner
at Burger King where we dine on chicken
fries & don paper crowns for a royal feel.

On another show date, I take two women into South
Dakota where fly we over the heads of white
slave owners carved into a sacred Native mountain.
At the end of the date, I offer no roses to either
woman & abandon them on a canopied bed
in the middle of the Badlands & take off
in a helicopter to provide the cameras
an aerial view of wilderness & despair.
At the end of the show, I find myself proposing
to a fertility nurse in a barn made to look
like a chapel & not the place where I raised
my first horse, fucked my first goat. Here,
I will milk the cows for our future offspring
to drink straight from the teat like I did as a kid.
The show ends & I rise from the couch
& walk into the kitchen. On bended knee,
I reach for a bottle of a beer deep
in the back of the fridge, pop the top
like a question & take a swig, cold
& crisp once it hits my full lips.

The Bachelor Attends a Gay Wedding

An outdoor affair in late July, the air moist
& primed for a downpour that never came.
Even though the invite said to dress for
the weather, I wrapped my body in the same
three-piece suit I'd worn to three straight weddings
the past year—a commitment to cloth & coin,
the only kind I'm capable of. Still,
my suit clung to my body like a damp towel,
warm & worn w/the dirt of days past.
During the ceremony, we heard tributes
& sniffles, an epithalamium from the mother
of the groom, un vals peruano de la madre
del novio. The open bar served drinks
w/names like The Wink, Horse's Neck,
The Fluffy Mel, Japanese Slipper. I sipped
too many cocktails to count & counted on
my guest brother, a sober confirmed bachelor,
to get us home. We met a man named Dr. Stitch,
a certified apparel technician, & his lover who wore
a vest full of faces. Dr. Stitch told me I have a long
torso. I wanted him to size me up, to seize
my shoulders & measure their width. I confessed
the suit was not mine but my body didn't mind
the way its seams seemed custom-made for my frame.
He gave me his card, said I should visit his clinic.
Throughout the day, I caught men glancing my way
& welcomed their gaze after nights of women
turning to look at their phones. When we said goodbye
to the grooms, I kissed them on the lips, felt
their facial hair brush against my own, bristle
upon bristle, their sweat clinging to my chin.

The Bachelor Eats Cheetos, Ponders Love on a Rooftop

for Megan Hammond

From up here, the half-moon appears graspable,
edible even—a slice of a blood orange
or the red curling finger of a Flamin' Hot
Cheeto. In order to reach it, I climb the cold
black ladder to the other level, the roof
over your roof, closer to the stars we can't see
beyond city lights smothering the view.
Maybe it's the chemical compound of Cheetos talking
but if I had a spaceship, I'd zoom us to the moon,
run my crimson-colored fingers through your hair
& offer you a strawberry-flavored Ring Pop
like the prop rose I see in *The Bachelor*
except I'm not white & you're not a princess
& this isn't a cut-and-paste paradise.
This is the view of a gritty, dirty city
from your rooftop but I want us to go higher,
in part because of the joint in my pocket,
in part because of the thawing my heart receives
from your radiance. I want us to marvel at the marble
of the half-moon, of which we see only half, anyway.
The other half lies hidden from our world's turning
on its fixed axis but I want us to access the parts
of a world where we could be alone drinking cheap sangria
straight from the bottle, burrow our hands into a bag
of fire & come out unscathed, our fingers clutching
a cluster of rubies & pearls. The possibility is silly
in the eyes of the skeptic but for this believer
it's more than mere whim or passing thought
like this plane flying overhead, closer now up here.
So close I'm willing to jump & grab hold of a wing
w/one hand, the other reaching back for yours.

The Bachelor Looks Up the Etymology of Bachelor

n. 1. Before 1300, from Old French *bacheler* meaning
a young man, of which I sort of am, young-ish
w/wisps of white hair on my head & beard
& a knee clicking w/each descending step
I take. 2. A young aspirant knight
or squire from the Arthur era. Could I be
a knight? Sir Boozer from the House Agave—
a surly warrior in iron armor too bulky
& burdensome for my slight frame,
my arms struggling to unsheath a sword
from a leather holster? I'm probably better
suited a squire fetching fresh water to drink
& snaring wild hares to skin & cook. I'd write
letters home on parchment scrolls inked
w/flawless calligraphy: *My Dear Lady Dreamsicle,*
The world outside the castle is rough & full of thieves
& drunks & whores who wish to give me syphilis.
Every night we make camp, I look up to the stars
& send a thousand kisses skyward, hoping the wind
guides them your way... 3. A university graduate
of the lowest degree, which I own, a Bachelor
of Arts from an unranked liberal arts college, sinking
in accreditation & debt each year. 4. An unmarried man,
which I am, unwed & identify as a cis-male.
Ultimately, the origin of *bachelor* is uncertain
similar to the origin of this bachelor—born
to a woman sleeping w/a man she assumed
a bachelor who moved to Tejano music w/ease
only he was separated from a wife while drinking
at bars & dancing w/a woman w/a history
of giving birth & signing her name as the Mother
w/the Father portion marked *unknown.*

The Bachelor Visits His Mother

She greets me/w a smooch & pinch
of my cheek, a smile to melt the glacier
my heart is buried in. Even though I'm wearing
a pair of basketball shorts & t-shirt straight
from the dirty pile & I haven't shaved
or trimmed any type of hair on my body
in weeks, she says I'm her handsome boy
& I believe her. She serves me a plate
of three tacos filled w/hamburger meat
& potatoes flavored w/the dust of chiles
not found in the depths of a Mexican jungle
guarded by a mystical man-eating jaguar
but in the Ethnic Foods aisle: a small packet
of taco seasoning sprinkled on the meat
like fairy dust, casting a spell on my palate
to create a taste muy authentico. This dinner
so much better than last night's combo
of chips & salsa & Chunky Monkey ice cream.
She works at a daycare my brothers & I call *Band-Aids*
for the wound of being the only one of her eight siblings
to have no grandkids yet. After giving birth
to four boys, two of which are confirmed bachelors
& the other married into a family already established,
my brothers call me the Last Hope.
I pour myself another drink. When she asks
about any dates, I do not mention the woman
who slept in my bed the other night & the burn
I now feel deep in my loins, which is not love.
My mother comments on the gray in my hair,
more than was there yesterday. She tells me
she has no plans to retire as she turns sixty-six.
She says she likes carrying around the babies

of other people even though her back hurts
& they all grow up & move into the toddler room.

III

Holding Court

Today I became King
of the Court w/out a diamond
encrusted crown thrust upon
my sweaty head. Instead
my markings of royalty
were the t-shirt draping
my body like a robe soaked
in champagne & the pain
in my right knee—a sign
of a battle endured, my will
tested & bested by none
as the ball flew off my hands
as swift as an arrow toward
the heart of a target—my fingers
ringless yet feeling like gold.

Lalo Rots

He was an Angel who preferred to swim
during hot summer days on Earth where
he hung out poolside wearing baggy trunks
that sunk below his waistline when wet,
offering a brush of puberty in bloom.

He could not hide the wings bursting
from his back in feathers of white
& royal blue—the colors of Latin Angels
everywhere. Sometimes he would let
little kids pluck a quill & they would kill
each other w/laughter in tickle fights.

Outside the pool, he cruised
the streets w/his boys in a lowrider
that bumped & humped the roads
in a hydraulic, hypnotic rhythm
in sync to beats of gangsta rap blasting
from speakers rattling the trunk.

He loved the skunky smell of hydro-
ponic weed leaking from windows
rolled down a crack to trap in
the smoke his boys coughed up.
He said Angel Dust is just a name
& nothing like the drugs found in Heaven—
real primo shit to bleed your eyes out.

A King w/a crooked gold crown drove by
the pool in a car riding low to ground
from the wear & tear of terrorizing

hoods not yet under his rule.
The King wanted to see a true Angel
take flight. He loaded up his car
w/pawns & guns & circled the block
twice before he unleashed a hail of words
claiming the hood his own while his boys
in the backseat slung bullets like arrows.

The Angel took a shot in the chest
& his flesh let loose a fury of blood
that oozed into the pool—a deep
red ink no chlorine could clean.
The other swimmers ran screaming
as car wheels screeched away, the exhaust
pipe backfiring a loud cough like a shot.

The Angel's boys vowed revenge
& warred w/the King who eluded
their bullets, their words, their intents
to topple his castle guarded by boys
who marked every hood & block
in black & gold crowns w/spray paint
hissing Lalo's name onto garage doors
& walls for all to see that there is no rest
for the dead, only a wilting decay.

Evolution of My Profile

Before, being bald & brown
badged me a 'banger:
black pants w/X color

shirt & head shaved short
branded me in X gang,
even if they hang in

a 'hood not my own,
I still got thrown on
a cop car's hood & trunk,

punched in the mouth
riding in a marked car
down the wrong streets.

Now, being brown & bearded,
on trains w/a backpack
bursting w/books,

I receive suspicious looks
from cops patrolling
w/bomb-sniffing dogs

as if I should be muzzled
& leashed like their animals—
collared & crated in the dark,

taught how to sit & lie
down & beg for treats,
only set free when I learn

not to bite back & snap
my jaw at the hand
petting my head.

Loteria

Nights of playing *Lotería*
w/Mom & Big Manny was a way
to learn the Spanish they spoke
to each other but not to us kids
who caught on to certain words
like *cállate, cerveza, chicharrón;*
little nuggets I ate up like pinto beans
we used to cover the board

instead of blue chips
Mom kept in her Bingo bag
she carried every Friday night
when her & Tia Shirley
went to the Moose Lodge,
her hair & coat reeking
w/the smoke of all who lost.

El Borracho, the man holding a bottle
& about to fall over yet never does
like Big Manny stumbling home
w/breath & belly full of beer,
bumbling into our bedroom
& letting loose a stream of piss
that splashed onto hardwood floors
to shake my brother and I awake.

La Garza, the heron dipping
a beak in water like cousin Tony rushing
back & forth from the bathroom
to sneak bumps of coke during a sleepover
w/pizza & Playstation on a 40-inch TV

& I rubbed numb my teenage
teeth when offered a taste.

El Músico, the chubby man clutching
his *guitarra* similar to my brother Dave gripping
a stack of vinyl to spin on a Technics
turntable case set up in the bedroom
where he practiced & I slept on the top
bunk bed until I fell off one night
& hit my back on a corner as sharp
& cold as his cut & scratch skills.

La Sirena w/her body emerging from water
like a buoy for a pubescent boy's memory
of her breasts free of seashells
she now holds to cover them
in water so blue & cold,
her scales red & glistening,
her name clung to the tongue
like *dulce de leche*.

Forged

My brother wore bags over his boots
      to keep the grease & grime from his time
            at the steel mill off the carpet & steps

he mounted, heaving each foot
      like a monster born of the grave
            -yard shift—stiff & awkward

his arms smeared w/dark matter,
      the lather of machine & industry
            bathing his clothes & face in a glaze

of sweat & smoke, oil & the dirt
      of what's been done before—the work
            of uncles & cousins who wore the same

jumpsuit, goggles & gloves to grab hold
      of cold finished bars using their backs
            & shoulders to move the weight around

w/the help of machines, the knobs
      to control the two-ton bundles
            held by a buckle above the heads

of hard hatted men that could snap
      & let loose the mass of all that metal
            meant to weld into a foundation

a beginning to build upon
      when it was his time to work
            to clock in clean & leave

feeling filthy no matter the shift
    or stiffness in the bones creaking
        like the wooden stairs he climbed

Traviesos

We pass a joint to one another under the cover
of hoodies & hairnets, our bodies perched on

Popeye's porch who's on the corner cracking jokes,
clinking bottles w/other boys in baggy black clothes

—troublemakers in the eyes of those who don't know
any better. You hit it hard & hold your breath—a sea

diver sinking into the dark crevices of a cave
& you hand me the wet end of a torch we hope

never extinguishes, the way our friendship will
years from now. In that passing, we hear a whistle

of metal & flame, a buzz in front of our faces. It takes
a moment for the coughing to kick in & our thoughts

clicking into place—shots coming from across the tracks
where figures in black & beige flash their hands in fury

w/the hurried tongue of taunt & war. We duck
under the stairs, a pair of scared fifteen year olds

waiting for the silence to begin, for their fingers to tire
of firing on boys who look just like them. When the shooting

stalls, we crawl out & I run across the street, up the steps
of my own porch while you take off towards Popeye,

your body disappearing around the curve.

Gang of the Dead

after George Romero

In the movies, it's better to be black
or brown when zombies hunger for
flesh, our bodies tested fighting a war
for plots of land always under attack.

Our primal instinct kicks in when we see
hordes of lumbering pale corpses
like conquistadores w/out horses
ready to enslave, craving the body.

We train for this growing up in gangs:
where to get guns, where to run & hide from
the dead like cops that want us in prison
or dead, not bred to fight back against clans.

We live thanks due to our blood & tribal,
savage ways of slaying for survival.

Doing Your Dead Father's Dishes

for Fred Sasaki

As I washed away the backwash
of your father's glass, the offering
plate for your grandmother's ashes
which held fruit so old & moldy
the apple & orange hardened
into a plastic feel & the last bits
of his spit clinging to a cold
metal spoon tongued smooth
of the ice cream it once scooped,
I thought I was cleaning my hands
w/his spittle & spirit, lathering
my skin w/the dust of his dead cells.

I know that's lurid & morbid to say,
maybe more than you care to bear
but my mother is still alive & my father
is unknown to me & could be a ghost
as well. Still I haven't had to clean
the kitchen of a lost loved one, to scrub
away the grime of leftovers, to strip
the bed of its sheets & pillows only
to see the yellow outline of what was
your father's sweat, the nights he turned
& twisted under the blanket feeling
the heat of dreams press onto his skull.

I imagine him waking from a hot sleep
& drinking a full glass of water in one
gulp for luck & constitution purposes.
I imagine him pulling back the curtains

to look onto the lake while stretching
the bones of his skeleton, his arms
reaching for ceiling, straining to gain
back the inches shed & lost, the light
of the sun flooding into his room
as it slowly rises over an expanse
of water blue & seemingly endless.

blue prick

what began as a drop
    of ink became a blot
        of blue bruised on

her wrist, not kissed on
    the way I romanticized it—
        an abandoned rosary or

rose to be wound around her
    radius bone like thorned ivy
        —but forced on by a former

lover, the one my brothers
    hinted at in hushed talks
        of homemade tattoos

at the kitchen table, wielder
    of needle & alcohol, swinger
        of a two-by-four to her

head, prodder of blood
    & tears on her face,
        maker of a scar veiled

under hair unlike the blue prick
    on skin—what was to be his
        initials—slapped on her wrist

Antisonnet

after Nicanor Parra

I would prefer to die ahead of you
& hope your heart bursts apart knowing
deep down what your dick did
dicking around my mom & sticking her
w/a kid you didn't bother to father
were just a fucker fucking around
on your wife who was not my mom
left w/my body & bastardized blood
I would kill to spill & so fill myself
w/drink & think you're dead
I think I'm drunk & hope you're sunk
in a coffin cutoff from the air we share
till death & if not dead then the desire:
I would prefer that you be first to die
        it's what parents do

Bookmark Found in *The Works of Walt Whitman*

As usual my brother & I are glass-eyed & smiles,
talking about our desire to stop smoking
when I pull the book off its shelf.
I brush some dust off Whitman's hat
& beard like ash, finger through pages
& find a bookmark courtesy of
the American Cancer Society.
"How appropriate," I say when I give it to him.
He sees the picture of a girl's face
with cheeks round as apples, eyes dark as tar
looking for a cure for cancer.
The caption under her face reads
Best Tip: Don't Start.
He laughs, accidentally loses his hit, flips
the bookmark over & reads
that smoking kills more people every year
than car crashes, AIDS & murders combined.
"Shit, if that ain't a wakeup call..."
he says as he tightly packs another bowl,
takes a deep puff & exhales
like an ancient dragon's last breath.

A Case of MGDs

I drank four MGDs Monday
        night because I smoked all
                my weed last weekend.

Tio Jesse likes MGD any day,
        time of week; says initials
                mean Mexican Getting

Drunk. He drinks w/Big Manny
        (who likes Bud) some mornings
                over their huevos con nopales

y salsa. Tio attends AA
        on Sundays just to cook
                pans of pancakes & sausages

for sobersides then splits
        a sixer w/Big Manny in return
                for the leftovers brought over.

Mom doesn't mind the food,
        just the drink of husband,
                brother, nephew, sons

like grandpa's picture framed
        & displayed in the living room—
                he sitting on a sofa, a Pabst

Blue Ribbon in his brown hands.

Sweeping the States

they move in swift on the Swift
Plants in six states & sift
through the faces to separate
the dark from the light

like meat & seat them in
the back of vans packed tight
like the product they pack
& who's to pick up the slack

the black & white can't cut it
so the beef stacks sell single
to feed the pack   the flock
who block passages & clog

the cogs of the machine   the process
not so swift to give & grant a wish
of a place   a stake in the land
handling the steaks for the rest

to take in   to sate the mouths
of the stock who have stock
in the business of beef & beef
with the brown who ground them

Poem for the Grandmother

My abuela poem is buried in San Benito
its roots & heart deep in Texas earth
where the soil breeds seeds of grapefruit
& tangerine using irrigation systems
the same way I use family stories
to water this poem to grow

My abuela poem lives in the minds
of my mother & brothers   their talk
of my infant body running to her open
arms   their talk of her talking & talking
to herself in Spanish as she cooked tacos
& caldo de pollo   as she swept & mopped
the floor she'd crawled across fooling
my brother into thinking play time & not
her way of reaching back to the voices
calling out in her head

My abuela poem is full of tropes:
a woman w/beady eyes
coke bottle glasses   pink rollers
in her hair like dynamite ready
to explode into brown curls
her hands digging into the wet
mass of masa, pressing
a flour tortilla into a holy O

Mi abuela poema is a bungled phrase tumbling
out my mouth   my tongue adjusts
to its taste on my palate like a paleta
de tamarindo—a flavor unfavored
by my American lick

Poem for the Mother

The freckles speckling your face
mark none of your sons,
skipped us whole & clean
save for the occasional mole
found on your youngest one's shoulder,
the birthmark kissed onto your second child's cheek.

As a kid I grabbed hold
of the moles on your face & neck,
handled them like pearls of earth.
You said it was payback for the times
you played w/grandma's when you were small.

I want to dye your hair back
to brown instead of the blonde
in a bottle you brew every
few months—the flowing
brunette I see in old photos
back when I had a tail
you bleached gold one summer
& it shimmered under sunlight.

I want someone to love me faults & all—
the cough in my chest, the throat
I put poison down, the swelling
in my heart, the squeeze these arms
can give because you gave them.

I want to find the freckles
& moles blooming on your skin
on a kid of my own & I want them to play

w/the flab under my arms the same way
I used to toy w/yours when I was a boy
& I'll call it payback.

Evolution of My Block

As a boy I bicycled the block
w/a brown mop-top falling
into a tail bleached blond,

gold-like under golden light,
like colors of Noble Knights
'banging on corners, unconcerned

w/the colors I bore—a shorty
too small to war with, too brown
to be down for the block.

White Knights became brown
Kings still showing black & gold
on corners now crowned,

the block a branch branded
w/la corona graffittied on
garage doors by the pawns.

As a teen, I could've beamed
the crown, walked in w/out
the beat down custom,

warred w/my cousin
who claimed Two-Six,
the set on the next block

decked in black & beige.
But I preferred games to gangs,
books to crooks wearing hats

crooked to the left or right
fighting for a plot, a block
to spot & mark w/blood

of boys who knew no better
way to grow up than throw up
the crown & be down for whatever.

Acknowledgements

I am grateful to the editors and readers of the following journals and books in which these poems first appeared (at times in different versions):

After Hours: "This Never Happened"

Columbia Poetry Review: "Cops & Robbers," "The Lot as Baseball Field," and "Mad About Cows"

The Economy: "Demon" (published as "Devil's Snack") and "Shootaround"

Great River Review: "*Lotería*" (published as "I Remember *Lotería*") and "Evolution of My Skin"

Jet Fuel Review: "Evolution of My Profile"

OCHO: "Chula"

PANK: "The Bachelor Takes Out the Trash" and "blue prick"

Pinwheel: "Lalo Rots"

Poetry: "The Bachelor Watches *The Bachelor*," "Evolution of My Block," "Forged," "GTA: San Andreas/Berwyn (or, 'Grove Street, bitch!')," "Holding Court" and "Sweeping the States"

RHINO: "Blue Line Incident"

Sonneteering: "Sonnet of the Dead" and "Gang of the Dead"

Spoon River Poetry Review: "The Bachelor Makes Dinner," "Bait," "Doing Your Dead Father's Dishes," "The Lot as Boxing Ring," "Poem for the Grandmother" and "Showering"

Tammy: "The Bachelor Eats Cheetos, Ponders Love on Rooftop" and "The Bachelor Visits His Mother"

TriQuarterly: "*Traviesos*"

"Sweeping the States" was reprinted in *The Open Door: 100 Poems, 100 Year of* Poetry *Magazine* Edited by Don Share and Christian Wiman (Chicago: University of Chicago Press, 2012)

"Evolution of My Block" and "GTA: San Andreas/Berwyn (or, 'Grove Street, bitch!')" was reprinted in *The BreakBeat Poets: New American Poetry in the Age of Hip-Hop* Edited by Kevin Coval, Quarysh Ali Lansana and Nate Marshall (Chicago: Haymarket Books, 2015)

Thank you to Don Share and Christian Wiman for awarding me a Ruth Lilly Poetry Fellowship in 2012. Thank you to staff of Poetry and the Poetry

Foundation, especially Holly Amos, Lindsay Garbutt, Katherine Litwin, Ydalmi Vanessa Noriega Pérez and Fred Sasaki (bro!). Your support over the years has been overwhelming.

Thank you to Francisco Aragón for providing me a Letras Latinas Residency Fellowship at the Anderson Center where I first drafted a version of the book. Thank you to Robert Hedin for advice and encouragement. Thank you to my fellow residents for making the experience memorable and magical: Angélica Minero Escobar, Micahel Tsalka, Tom Virigin, Martina Stock, Chris Keming, Nick Healy and Sarah Fox (Tower Queen!).

Thank you to Mary Hawley, Mike Puican and the Guild Complex for years of support.

Thank you to the Columbia College Chicago Creative Writing department and the Library. Thank you to my teachers Arielle Greenberg, Tony Trigilio, David Trinidad and Ed Roberson. Thank you to the library staff for support and being such great coworkers.

Thank you to CantoMundo for support, inspiration and building a community of Latinx poetry.

Thank you my RHINO family/crash/herd. I'm grateful to be in your company and am in awe of your love and knowledge of poetry. Much love to you all!

Thank you to Natalie Hill, Kimiko Ostrozovich Garbe, Daniel Suárez and Chris Zdenek for friendship and workshop outside of the workshop.

Shout out to my Latin Immortal Gangstas: Juan Carillo, Victor Garcia, Carlos Pizarro and Paul Pizarro. We've all come a long way from 15th and 51st Ave.

Shout out to my brothers from other mothers Tom Franklin and Stan Brown. Triple Threat 4 Life!

Thank you to Ralph Hamilton, Katie Hartsock, Erika L. Sánchez, Elizabeth Stigler and Angelica Narciso Torres who provided invaluable feedback on various drafts of the manuscript. Thank you to Kyle Churney for feedback and for throwing me the title/crown.

Thank you to Krista Franklin for providing a beautiful cover art. I am grateful for your reading of the book and am in awe of your talents.

Thank you to Gregory Pardlo for seeing and believing in my work. I will be forever grateful and indebted to you. Thank you to Elizabeth Scanlon, American Poetry Review and the Honickman Foundation for the recognition and support. Thank you Copper Canyon Press for giving my book a home.

Thank you to Megan Hammond for love and light and support.

Lastly, thank you to my family, my mother and brothers, for unconditional love and support and believing in my writing since I was kid filling notebooks with sci-fi and fantasy stories then, later, poetry. Thank you to all my tíos and tías, my primos and primas, the memory of grandparents and ancestors. We can't choose our family but I'm blessed to have been born into the Castillo clan.

About the Author

Jacob Saenz is a CantoMundo fellow whose work has appeared in *Pinwheel, Poetry, Tammy, Tri-Quarterly* and other journals. He's been the recipient of a Letras Latinas Residency Fellowship as well as a Ruth Lilly Poetry Fellowship. He serves as an associate editor for *RHINO*.